ARE YOU A LEADER?

Keys to unlocking your potential

ADEOLA BABATUNDE

Acknowledgement

Special thanks to my wife (Bola) and Children(David, Daniel and Debbie) who gave me the time and space to write.

To the authors and teachers I have learnt from, for their guidance and support along the way

To my clients who allowed me to share what I have learnt through relating with them.

==

For more information about this publication, send your mail to :

info@adeolababatunde.com

Printed in the United States of America

© Adeola Babatunde 2014

www.adeolababatunde.com

info@adeolababatunde.com

ISBN 978-1-326-00879-6

Published by:

David Daniel consultancy Ltd

CONTENTS

Introduction

Reading leadership literature you'd sometimes think that it was written in the stars that everyone has the potential to be an effective leader. I don't believe that to be true. In fact, I see way fewer truly effective leaders than I see people stuck in positions of leadership who are woefully incompetent at worst and seriously misguided about their own abilities at best.

Part of the reason this happens is a lack of honest self-assessment by those who aspire to leadership in the first place. To paraphrase a certain comedian, "you might be a potential leader if..."

You lead only when you have to, not all the time. We've all met the type of individual who simply must take charge. Whether it's a strategic brainstorming session, a pick-up basketball game, or a family outing, they can't help grabbing the lead dog position and clinging on to it for dear life.

Always opinionated, usually impatient and frequently brusque, these got to-be-in-fronters get so used to other people describing them as natural born leaders that sooner or later, to their own and everyone else's detriment, they begin to believe it.

Truth is they're most always nothing of the sort. True leaders don't presume that it's their divine right to take charge every time two or more people get together. Quite the opposite. A great leader will assess each situation on its merits, and will only take charge when their position, the situation, and/or the needs of the moment demand it.

Oh, and if you read that last paragraph with a sneaking belief that in most situations you *are* the right person to take charge, you're most likely a got to-be-in-fronter, not a leader.

You *see* much more than you do. Many business executives confuse leadership with action. These Tasmanian Devils believe that constant motion somehow generates leadership as a by-product. Consequently, the more ambitious they are for a leadership role, the more furious their momentum becomes.

Leaving us mere mortals in their wake, the Tasmanian devil works harder, faster, and longer than everyone else. Faced with any situation that can't be solved by the sheer brute force of activity, they generate a dust cloud of impatience. Their one leadership tool is volume: if they think you aren't working as hard as they are, or as hard as they think you should, their demands become increasingly louder and more strident.

You'd think that such a blunt, one-club-fits-all mentality would preclude our action-at-all-costs executive from attaining any degree of seniority in a mature organisation, but you'd be wrong. Sadly, many organisations, some of them Fortune 100 companies, encourage just such a chest-beating, fire-aim-ready definition of leadership. True leaders understand the value of action. Of course, but it isn't their only tool. In fact, it isn't even their primary tool. Great leaders seemore than everyone else: answers, solutions, patterns, problems, opportunities, threats. They know it's vitally important to do, but they also know that thinking, understanding, contemplation and interpretation are equally important.

You change people. They achieve outcomes. Executive A hits his targets and burns out his team in the process. Executive B builds a great team, but they miss their goal. Which is the better leader?

It's a false dichotomy and sadly, one that I see in organisations all the time. A true leader is option C: someone who develops his or her team so that they canand do hit their targets, achieve their goals.

If you're fixated on outcomes to the extent that you manipulate and bully others to achieve those outcomes (I know, you call it motivation--it isn't), then you aren't leading at all, you're dictating. And don't think this means that being a door mat is leadership either .True leadership means building strong, capable teams that are goal, achievement oriented.

Your thinking skills can be considered directional skills because they set the direction for your organisation. They provide vision, purpose, and goal definition. These are your eyes and ears to the future, allowing you to recognise the need for change, when to make it, how to implement it and how to manage it. You find a vision by reaching for any available reason to change, grow and improve. Just as you perform preventive maintenance on your car, you must perform preventive maintenance on your organisation. Do not believe in the old adage, "If it isn't broke, don't fix it", for the people who do, go broke! Treat every project as a change effort. Treat every job as a new learning experience. Good organisations convey a strong vision of where they will be in the future. As a leader, you have to get your people to trust you and be sold on your vision. Using the leadership tools described in this guide and being honest and fair in all you do will provide you with the 'ammo' you need to gain their trust. To sell them on your vision, you need to possess energy and display a positive attitude that is contagious. People want a strong vision of where they are going. No one wants to be stuck in a dead-end company going nowhere ... or a company headed in the wrong direction. They want to be involved with a winner! And your people are the ones who will get you to that goal. You cannot do it alone!

When setting goals, keep these points in mind:

They should be realistic and attainable.

They should improve the organisation (morale, monetary, etc.).

As many people as possible should be involved in the goal-setting process (they will feel a sense of ownership that will drive them to achieve it).

A process should be developed to achieve each goal

WHAT IS LEADERSHIP?

Leadership, and the study of it, has roots in the beginning of civilisation. Egyptian rulers, Greek heroes and biblical patriarchs all had one thing in common – leadership. There are numerous definitions and theories of leadership; however, there are enough similarities in the definitions to conclude that leadership is an effort of influence and the power to induce compliance (Wren, 1995). Our work, work environment, the motivation to work, leaders, leadership, leadership style, and a myriad of other work-related variables have been studied for almost two centuries.

The organisational focus of the leader has evolved over this same period. Early organisations with authoritarian leaders, who believed employees were intrinsically lazy, transitioned into ways to make work environments more conducive to increased productivity rates. Today, organisations are transforming into places where people are empowered, encouraged, and supported in their personal and professional growth throughout their careers. As the focus of leaders has changed over time, it has influenced and shaped the development and progression of leadership theory.

Leadership is the art of motivating a group of people to act towards achieving a common goal.

This definition of leadership, I think, captures the leadership essentials of inspiration and preparation. Effective leadership is based upon ideas, but won't happen unless those ideas can be communicated to others in a way that engages them.

Put even more simply, the leader is the inspiration and director of the action. He is the person in the group that possesses the combination of personality and leadership skills that makes others want to follow his direction.

In business, leadership is welded to performance. Those who are viewed as effective leaders are those who increase their company's bottom lines.

To further confuse the definition of leadership, we tend to use the terms "leadership" and "management" interchangeably, referring to a

Company's management structure as its leadership or to individuals who are actually managers as the "leaders" of various management teams.

I am not saying that this is a bad thing; just pointing out that leadership involves more. To be effective, a leader certainly has to manage the resources at her disposal. But leadership also involves communicating, inspiring and supervising - just to name three more of the primary leadership skills a leader has to have to be successful.

Is a leader born or made? While there are people who seem to be naturally endowed with more leadership abilities than others, I believe that people can learn to become leaders by improving particular leadership skills.

-1-

Who is a Leader?

At the most basic level, a leader is someone who leads other. But what makes someone a leader? What is it about being a leader that some people understand and use to their advantage? What can you do to be a leader? Here's what you need to know and do.

A leader is a person who has a vision, a drive and a commitment to achieve that vision, and the skills to make it happen. Let's look at each of those in detail.

If your actions inspire others to dream more, learn more, do more and become more, you are a leader.

When we hear people talk about leadership, many people think national politics, parliaments, and other big public positions but leadership does not begin there.

It begins in our homes, schools, work places, communities to name but a few. Leadership is not about holding lofty positions and enjoying the perks?

It is about the ability to lead and therefore serve the people as opposed to ruling servants. Leadership is more about servitude and less about control.

It is not uncommon for some individual to seek positions and titles and then seek to use those positions and titles to exert their influence on their juniors forcefully. These people are eager to be called the "boss."

They want authority to be derived from their position for the sake of their title instead of painstakingly building that authority through mutual respect and clear rational thinking and decision-making in the process of serving those they are meant to lead.

The history of the world is strewn with individuals who have sought to rule instead of lead by the use of forceful coercion to exert submission to their sense of leadership. But true leadership comes from within.

If an individual stands in a workplace meeting and says that we need to give each other due respect because we are all worthy of this respect for the effort we put in the organisation, people will believe him if he is seen to respect his peers, his juniors and his seniors in equal measure. But if the person in question is the leader of hooliganism, gossip and corrupting behaviour, his workmates will seldom believe in him.

Just as leadership, in the twenty first century, genuine authority is earned not demanded.

A person in a position of authority should be able to exude respectful behaviour and in effect earn his fellow peers' respect.

A good leader must not demand obedience from his subjects but must be able to demonstrate an ability to draw obedience without demanding it by exemplifying fairness and good judgment irrespective of social classes or standards.

A leader who demands obedience or authority as opposed to drawing it from his subjects who in this case he is supposed to serve is lacking of personal humility and respect or may lack the ability to inspire the people around them to be better and hence will reduce to issuing orders.

The environment today favours kings of persuasion as opposed to the use of power or force to get things done. Politics is basically a battle to persuade the voter that you are the best person to get the job done. Whether you are the best or not does not affect your ability to win apart from the perception that the voter gets of you. So is advertising. It's all about image.

An old spite advert that ascertained that "Image is everything", is spot on.

Corporate leaders don't only need to understand strategy but also have to be able to inspire their sales and managerial terms into believing that they can do the job at hand.

More and more companies are encouraging creative environments where employees are encouraged to think innovatively and harness ideas for progress.

Hence the leader's role changes from issuing orders to creating conducive environment for ideas to flourish and to direct the creative flow in a direction that will maintain business growth avoid over-scattering of ideas and create an all-inclusive atmosphere.

Creative people require less control and more guidance and encouragement. Control stifles the mind while encouragement and guidance breeds ideas.

What is the difference between a Boss and a Leader?

A boss is that individual that supervises his or her employees. He watches them to make sure they're working and on task. At his worst, the Boss treats his employees like lowly servants. At his best, he gets the job done but goes no further. He has no interest in bettering his employees, encouraging them to take training courses or improve themselves: <u>A boss is not a teacher.</u>

While…

A leader is a motivator. He takes time to build teams of people who respect him.

A leader must listen, learn and respect the opinions of others. No one ever learned anything by talking. Make your staff feel involved, and they will buy into your goals and aspirations, you will get where you are trying to go much quicker and with less friction. Does this mean that you should only listen and take advice from your top executives and advisors? Absolutely not.

Leader	Boss
Inspires employees	Drives employees
Depends on respect and honour	Depends on authority
Cares for your well-being	Cares for your productivity level
Says 'We'	Says 'I'
Inspires enthusiasm	Inspires fear
Gives credit	Takes credit
Says 'Let's go'	Says 'Go'
Asks	Orders
Knows how it is done	Shows how it is done

What is one of the most important tools a leader can have? Extensive training, a handful of certificates, or an impressive resume maybe? Surprisingly, all these things pale in comparison to one tool no leader should be without, a positive mental attitude.

That's right, having a positive mental attitude determines how you experience your life. In turn, it determines how you behave as a leader and the influence you have on others. We have talked before about smiling and the positive to negative ratio - so this information shouldn't come as a surprise to you.

When you smile, you make others happy. When you concentrate on being the positive factor in your team's day, their productivity goes up. When you seek out good things to say about others, you will find more good things about them. This is not coincidental. This is the power of being positive. I know sometimes that can seem like an impossible task.

With all the worries and stresses of today, staying positive might not be at the top of your to do list. You hear everyone speak of the down economy, you watch horrors on the news, and you may have lay-offs or shut-downs in your company. I am certainly not saying staying positive isn't a challenge sometimes. However, as leaders . . . should we not rise to the challenge? You don't need to be unrealistically upbeat, just try to remember that you can affect a lot more than you think by adjusting your perception.

Your attitude has the power to not only lift you up or pull you down, but affect your team in the same way. Look for the positives in situations. Remember, as the saying goes, you need "to accept the things I cannot change, and the courage to change the things I can". You simply need the wisdom to know the difference between the two. Try hard to focus on only the things you can directly influence. Work at making a positive difference on those things. Every day seek out new ways to keep yourself positive and new positive people to be around.

Remember, "Every day may not be good, but there is something good in every day." What good will you find today?

Do you have the *"right"* attitude? The right attitude is one of the most important characteristics that a good leader must possess. It makes all the difference between being effective out of respect and just being respected because it is your job title that demands it. Of course it is your choice about how you wish to look at things. If you want to achieve real success as a leader, it is imperative that you have the right attitude.

There are many challenges that a leader faces in the workplace. You must be able to successfully tackle the challenges if you have the right mind set. You must be able to alter your behaviour and influence others to give and be their very best all the time. A wrong decision can quickly kill morale and turn valuable stakeholders–including talented employees and customers away. By making changes to your thought processes, you can make that positive difference and help your organisation be as strong as it can be, no matter your position. You alone can grow your job security and help others grow theirs.

Team members do not whole-heartedly follow a leader who has a bad attitude. It can be quite challenging to have the right frame of mind when you are faced with problems at work. Stress can sometimes be a motivator. However, in the long-run if you are the cause of that stress, you can guarantee that employees are not really giving their best and may be looking for the first opportunity to jump ship. Yes, you may be the problem and getting only short-term results. However with the right attitude, you may be able to bounce back from the challenges, if you face them confidently. You can earn the respect of your followers on a new day if you maintain the attitude that the best leaders possess every day.

Tell me a leader who rejects every suggestion his team gives because he is afraid they cannot make it and I will tell you someone who is not fit to be a leader. Let me quote John Maxwell on how he views positive attitude. In his book, Developing the Leader within You, he says, "A positive attitude is one of the most valuables assets a person can have in life." It can help you achieve things that may seem impossible to happen.

As a leader, you will need more than a miracle to make certain things happen. As long as you have the right attitude of looking at things and on how they have to be done, you can eliminate the miracle wishing part. Most of the time, we become discouraged by how difficult the problems we face are. What we do not know is that it is not really the problems that are difficult to deal with but our attitude towards them. Yes, they may be tough at times and may take a lot of time to solve. But as long as we view them as obstacles that will hinder our way towards our goal, we can never really arrive at the right solution. Why don't we see these problems as challenges…as something to spice our journey up? Not all roads to success are smooth. Often, there are bumps and humps. If we miss our turn, we might get lost and end up starting all over again. See the big picture. Look beyond the problem. A positive leader will not dwell on a difficult situation and be discouraged by it, but will believe that he can and he ought to surpass it in order to reach his goals. With positive attitude, he never accepts defeat. Instead, he fights the noble battle until the very end.

Believing that you can make something happen is not at all a small thing when you put faith in yourself and believe that you can do it. What the mind says, the body will follow. It is a chain reaction.

When people see that their leader believes and strives hard for accomplishing a task, they will do the same. Imagine, if a single believer can make something happen, then how much more things can a team of believers bring out? Bringing Out the Positive Person in You

Ok, so you always see the glass half-empty. But you know what? Even if half of the water spills on the floor, it still contains water…and it is half full! Now how can you still see the good things in everything…even if you are pessimistic all the time?

7 Simple Tips to improve the attitude of leaders

1. **Positive Attitude**: Leaders who have a positive attitude are able to make a big difference to the organisation and the workforce they lead. If you want others to be positive, you need to reflect that change. You must get rid of negativity and find things that build your self-confidence.

2. **Think of every challenge as an opportunity.** You need to remind yourself of the good things that you have accomplished by having a positive attitude. This needs to be done when faced with crisis. This will help you regain confidence and self-belief.

3. **Have confidence, so others will believe in you.** Your team members will be willing to follow your lead, if you have the right

attitude. Do not give others reason to doubt you. Believe in yourself first, it will give others confidence in you too. This can be contagious and people will start admiring this quality when you are upbeat even during discouraging circumstances. You need to believe that you can do it and this will help you achieve success irrespective of what you do.

4. **Think win-win**. Create an environment that is open to the ideas of others, by showing others that you want everyone to feel and be winners. It is all about an attitude of thinking win-win. Make an effort to improve the environment at the workplace. This will help in conflict resolution and you would be able to improve productivity. When others think of what will be a positive outcome for others first, then everyone will try to help each other be and feel successful. You get to shape that environment.

5. **See failures and opportunities for improvement.** Face it; we all make mistakes–even you. Your attitude will determine how successful you are in your chosen career. All leaders go through their share of setbacks and it is important that you have confidence in your abilities so that you are able to face such setbacks. You need to learn from your failures and move forward. Dwelling on failures does nothing positive if you don't see them as opportunities to grow and do things differently. Others will quickly embrace this winning attitude, if you model it first.

6. **Own your mistakes and don't make others feel bad for errors.** Take personal responsibility for your work and do not try to pass the blame. You will earn the respect of others when you are always truthful and never lie about anything. Making mistakes is a human thing. It is not what happens, but how you handle things that truly matters. Nobody can afford to have questionable

character. Your reputation is earned and you shape it one action at a time.

7. **Have the attitude of gratitude.** Always show others that you are sincerely thankful for what they bring to the workplace. Say thank you in a meaningful way—with sincerity and specifics of what you are thankful for. Smile at others and be kind. It is respectful and helps set a positive tone that is contagious. Remember the leader shapes the work environment every day and at every moment. Of course anyone can be seen as a leader just by going above and beyond. Saying thankful and being thankful really can make a positive difference!

Your attitude not just affects you but also that of your team. You get to choose your own attitude and when you keep yourself positive, you are better able to achieve the goals and objectives of your organisation more easily. Truly, your attitude has a direct effect on how far you can go in your career. Help others feel and be their very best. Choose a positive attitude all the time. Everyone must be positive and any negativity from any team member can take a negative effective on others. Keep it positive.

When you start looking at things in an optimistic manner, you are better able to perform to the best of your potential—even in adverse circumstances. You must always practice having a good attitude so that it becomes part of your personality. Others will subconsciously model their attitudes and behaviours on what they see from the leader.

-2-

The Leader's Vision

A leader has a vision. Leaders see a problem that needs to be fixed or a goal that needs to be achieved. It may be something that no one else sees or simply something that no one else wants to tackle. Whatever it is, it is the focus of the leader's attention and they attack it with a single-minded determination.

Whether the goal is to double the company's annual sales, develop a product that will solve a certain problem, or start a company that can achieve the leader's dream, the leader always has a clear target in mind. This is a big picture sort of thing, not the process improvement that reduces errors by 2% but the new manufacturing process that completely eliminates the step that caused the errors. It is the new product that makes people say "why didn't I think of that", not just a toaster that lets you select the degree of darkness of the toast. Edison did not set out to build a better candle; he wanted to find a whole new way to illuminate the darkness. That's the kind of vision a leader has.

The Drive to See It through

It is not enough to just have a vision. Lots of people see things that should be done, things that should be fixed, great step forward that could be taken. What makes leaders different is that they act. They take the steps to achieve their vision.

Is it a passion for the idea, an inner sense of drive, or some sense of commitment? Whatever it is, it is the strength that lets leaders move their vision forward despite all the obstacles, despite all the people saying it can't be done, it's too costly; we tried that before, or a dozen other excuses. The true leader perseveres and moves forward.

Every business needs an effective leader. Highly effective leadership is rare. Here's my checklist, which comes from helping hundreds of CEOs, entrepreneurs and managers become more effective leaders.

The top 10 characteristics of an effective Leader

1. Is Truly humble - Leads to Serve: No one likes to work for a jerk or buy from a jerk. If you are obsessed with your own self-image, you will be your own worst enemy. Most CEOs and entrepreneurs are helpful people. For every Larry Ellison, there are millions, of nice-guy/gal business leaders whose good character makes people want to associate with them.A real leader lives to help others.

2. Is Non-Judgmentally Observant: If you observe your own behaviour non-judgmentally, but with the constant desire to improve, you will get much farther than if you berate yourself, or excuse or justify your shortcomings. You will also be a dispassionate listener. It will be more difficult for others to guess what you're thinking, and they will be more likely to tell you more. Everyone who works for you should know that, what you're really interested in is the facts.

You will also objectively observe other aspects of their behaviour and character - including how they treat those below them, how much they contribute to the solution (rather than being part of the problem), how much others respect them, how competitive or cooperative they are, how observant they are of others, how much they include others, and so on. Being a calm observer will help you see these behaviours more clearly.

3. Faces and Solves Problems: Once the good leader is satisfied that she has uncovered the truth, she then sets out to solve the problem. She doesn't procrastinate or spend too much time gathering unnecessary additional data. She gets the right people involved right away, she tells them what she has observed, tells them what she's decided to do so far, and then works with them to solve the problem. Ineffective CEOs decide that it's personal, and invest their energy in "taking offense."

They may simply refuse to acknowledge there's a problem. Even if they do acknowledge it, they may decide to ignore it, push it off on to someone else to fix or blame someone else for causing it, then fail to do anything about it. They may also pretend they are solving the problem when they are doing nothing about it.

The best employees and partners will try to help this CEO do the right thing. If their efforts fail, they will start looking around for new opportunities. As soon as they have found one, they will leave.

4. Ruthlessly Improves: The best leaders are ruthless about improvement. They are constantly finding new ways to educate their customers, employees, and partners. They are always looking at their processes, policies, and systems, and asking themselves: "How could we make this more efficient? What don't we need anymore? What do we need now?"

They don't fall into the "we've always done it this way" trap, which causes far too many companies to struggle - and fail.

5.Is Fiscally Conservative: I've seen some spectacular company failures. They all had one thing in common: They overspend. They manage to get some outside funding - either from venture capital or over-inflated stock prices - and they spend like there is no tomorrow. They are right - ultimately, for these companies, there *is* no tomorrow.

A good leader will think twice and will keep asking himself, "Do we need this now? Is there a less-expensive way of doing this?"

6. Invests in the Business: Even in a terrible economy, a good leader will invest in the business. She will just choose her investments wisely. The goal is to invest where it will have the most impact on revenue growth.

I recently interviewed a number of salespeople for a client who sells a very complex software programme. I ended up recommending that they increase education for their salespeople, so they can answer more of the customer's technical questions during the early discussions. Doing this will shorten the sales cycle, which will definitely have a positive effect on revenue growth.

7. Communicate Regularly, Clearly, and Purposefully: Effective leaders communicate regularly, clearly, and purposefully. Because they have been humble and objective enough to get the real story. Whatever they say rings true to those hearing it. The listeners are open to whatever comes next - a solution or a new directive. If a leader has obviously misread the signs, or has been misled, those listening will know it - and will not buy into his "solution."

Communication is not just about talking and writing. It's also about behaviour and character. If you say one thing and behave differently, your character will come into question. For example, a CEO may repeatedly say that he cares about employees, but never fraternise with them.

Once people start to get suspicious of your character, they will no longer follow. They will hold back, question your motives and integrity.

8. Gives Clear Direction: The effective leader works out how a project should proceed, then presents the plan in a well-organised, logical fashion that is easy for his customers, employees, or partners to understand and act upon.

He doesn't ramble on, verbally or in emails. He doesn't "think out loud." He doesn't rant. He doesn't berate anyone (especially in front of others), except in the very rare instance when it is entirely appropriate to do so.

Ranting is a data dump that satisfies the ego of the person ranting without benefiting those who must suffer through it - and then try to solve the problems anyway, as best they can. They will hesitate to come to that manager with new issues, because they won't want to sit through another harangue.

9. Evolves aggressively: A good leader knows that the company's products or services won't be in demand forever. He doesn't spend any time trying to imaginewhat the market will need next; guessing always invites disaster. Instead, he keeps his finger on the pulse of the customer's world. The minute the customer feels a need and starts to make a shift, he's thinking about how he can best meet that need.

He learns everything he can about it - *from customers*. His interviews will either convince him that it's only a passing fad, or that it's a real trend - and if it's a trend, he starts working immediately to see how his company can help customers meet their needs in that area. He starts with his*current* product offerings. Can they be repositioned? Repackaged? Reprised? Redesigned?

He doesn't set the whole company running off in a new direction, abandoning all the good things that everyone is already doing. But he does allocate resources to start meeting the new need and generating new revenue.

The effective leader becomes a valued and trusted partner for his customers, opening the door for him to introduce new products and services to them. They'll be more likely to buy from his company when something new is introduced, because the earlier products and services met their needs so well.

10. Has a Sense of Humour: Running a company is serious business, but if you can't laugh once in a while, you're not going to be an effective leader. A little wit goes a long way; no one considers a clown a leader. Light-hearted, self-deprecating humour works best. You should be able to laugh about your weaknesses, while constantly working to eliminate those weaknesses.

Bonus Characteristic:

11. Is Customer-Centric: The most effective leaders don't assume they know more than their customers. In my experience, these assumptions are always wrong. They ask their customers what they're thinking, using a method that will extract the maximum amount of actionable information with the least amount of effort.

5 most important Leadership traits

1. Honest
2. Forward-Looking
3. Competent
4. Inspiring
5. Intelligent

Your skill at exhibiting these five leadership qualities is strongly correlated with people's desire to follow your lead. Exhibiting these traits will inspire confidence in your leadership. Not exhibiting these traits or exhibiting the opposite of these traits will decrease your leadership influence with those around you. It is important to exhibit, model and display these traits. Simply possessing each trait is not enough; you have to display it in a way that people notice. People want to see that you actively demonstrate these leadership qualities and will not just assume that you have them. It isn't enough to just be neutral. For example, just because you are not dishonest will not cause people to recognise that you are honest. Just avoiding display of incompetence won't inspire the same confidence as truly displaying competence.

The focus of each of these five traits needs to be on what people see you do–not just the things they don't see you do. Being honest isn't a matter of not lying–it is taking the extra effort to display honesty.

Honesty as a Leadership Quality; People want to follow an honest leader. Years ago, many employees started out by assuming their leaders were honest simply because of the authority of their position. With modern scandals, this is no longer true.

When you start in a leadership position, you need to assume that people will think you are a little dishonest. In order to be seen as an honest individual, you will have to go out of your way to display honesty. People will not assume you are honest simply because you have never been caught lying.

One of the most frequent places where leaders miss an opportunity to display honesty is in handling mistakes. Much of a leader's job is to try new things and refine the ideas that don't work. However, many leaders want to avoid failure to the extent that they don't admit when something did not work.

There was a medium size organisation that was attempting to move to a less centralised structure. Instead of one location serving an entire city, they wanted to put smaller offices throughout the entire metro area. At the same time, they were planning an expansion for headquarters to accommodate more customers at the main site. The smaller remote offices were heralded as a way to reach more customers at a lower cost and cover more demographic areas.

After spending a considerable amount of money on a satellite location, it became clear that the cost structure would not support a separate smaller office. As the construction was completed on the expanded headquarters building, the smaller office was closed. This was good decision making. The smaller offices seemed like a good idea, but when the advantages didn't materialise (due to poor management or incorrect assumptions) it made sense to abandon the model. This was a chance for the leadership to display honesty with the employees, be candid about why things didn't work out as expected, learn from the mistakes and move on.

Unfortunately in this situation the leadership told employees that they had planned on closing the satellite location all along and it was just a temporary measure until construction was completed on the larger headquarters building. While this wasn't necessarily true, it didn't quite cross over into the area of lying. Within a few months the situation was mostly forgotten and everyone moved on. Few of the employees felt that leadership was being dishonest. However, they had passed up a marvellous opportunity to display the trait of honesty in admitting a mistake.

Opportunities to display honesty on a large scale may not happen every day. As a leader, showing people that you are honest even when it means admitting to a mistake, displays a key trait that people are looking for in their leaders. By demonstrating honesty with yourself, with your organisation and with outside organisations, you will increase your leadership influence. People will trust someone who actively displays honesty–not just as an honest individual, but as someone who is worth following.

Forward-Looking as a Leadership Trait

The whole point of leadership is figuring out where to go from where you are now. While you may know where you want to go, people won't see that unless you actively communicate it with them. Remember, these traits aren't just things you need to have, they are things you need to actively display to those around you. When people do not consider their leader forward-looking, that leader is usually suffering from one of two possible problems:

The leader doesn't have a forward-looking vision.

The leader is unwilling or scared to share the vision with others.

When a leader doesn't have a vision for the future, it is usually because they are spending so much time on today, that they haven't really thought about tomorrow. On a very simplistic level this can be solved simply by setting aside some time for planning, strategizing and thinking about the future. Many times when a leader has no time to think and plan for the future, it is because they are doing a poor job of leading in the present. They have created an organisation and systems that rely too much on the leader for input at every stage.

Some leaders have a clear vision, but don't wish to share it with others. Most of the time they are concerned that they will lose credibility if they share a vision of the future that doesn't come about. This is a legitimate concern. However, people need to know that a leader has a strong vision for the future and a strong plan for going forward. Leaders run into trouble sharing their vision of the future when they start making promises to individuals. This goes back to the trait of honesty. If a leader tells someone that "next year I'm going to make you manager of your own division", that may be a promise they can't keep. The leader is probably basing this promotion on the organisation meeting financial goals, but the individual will only hear the personal promise.

Long ago, an organisation was floundering. It seemed like everyone had a different idea about what they were trying to achieve. Each department head was headed in a different direction and there was very little synergy as small fiefdoms and internal politics took their toll.

Eventually a consulting firm was called in to help fix the problem. They analysed the situation, talked to customers, talked to employees and set up a meeting with the CEO. They were going to ask him about his vision for the future. The employees were excited that finally there would be a report stating the direction for the organisation.

After the meeting, the consultants came out shaking their heads. The employees asked how the important question had gone to which the consultants replied, "we asked him, but you aren't going to like the answer". The CEO had told the consultant that, while he had a vision and plan for the future, he wasn't going to share it with anyone because he didn't want there to be any disappointment if the goals were not reached.

Leaders can communicate their goals and vision for the future without making promises that they may not be able to keep. If a leader needs to make a promise to an individual, it should be tied to certain measurable objectives being met. The CEO in the example didn't realise how much damage he was doing, not demonstrating the trait of being forward-looking by communicating his vision with the organisation.

The CEO was forward-looking. He had a plan and a vision and he spent a lot of time thinking about where the organisation was headed. However, his fear of communicating these things to the rest of the organisation hampered his leadership potential.

Competency as a Leadership Quality

People want to follow someone who is competent. This doesn't mean a leader needs to be the foremost expert on every area of the entire organisation, but they need to be able to demonstrate competency.

For a leader to demonstrate that they are competent, it isn't enough to just avoid displaying incompetency. Some people will assume you are competent because of your leadership position, but most will have to see demonstrations before deciding that you are competent.

When people under your leadership look at some action you have taken and think, "that just goes to show why he is the one in charge", you are demonstrating competency. If these moments are infrequent, it is likely that some demonstrations of competency will help boost your leadership influence.

Like the other traits, it isn't enough for a leader to be competent. They must demonstrate competency in a way that people notice. This can be a delicate balance. There is a danger of drawing too much attention to yourself, in a way that makes the leader seem arrogant. Another potential danger is that of minimizing other people's contributions and appearing to take credit for the work of others.

As a leader, one of the safest ways to "toot you own horn without blowing it", is to celebrate and bring attention to team achievements. In this way you indirectly point out your competency as a leader.

Inspiration as a Leadership Trait

People want to be inspired. In fact, there is a whole class of people who will follow an inspiring leader–even when the leader has no other qualities. If you have developed the other traits in this book, being inspiring is usually just a matter of communicating clearly and with passion. Being inspiring means telling people how your organisation is going to change the world.

A great example of inspiration is when Steve Jobs stole the CEO from Pepsi by asking him, "Do you want to sell sugar water for the rest of your life, or do you want to change the world?" Being inspiring means showing people the big picture and helping them see beyond a narrow focus and understand how their part fits into the big picture.

One technique to develop your ability to inspire is telling stories. Stories can be examples from your customers, fictitious examples from your customers or even historical fables and myths. Stories can help you vividly illustrate what you are trying to communicate. Stories that communicate on an emotional level help communicate deeper than words and leave an imprint much stronger than anything you can achieve through a simple stating of the facts.

Learning to be inspiring is not easy–particularly for individuals lacking in charisma. It can be learned. Take note of people who inspire you and analyse the way they communicate. Look for ways to passionately express your vision. While there will always be room for improvement, a small investment in effort and awareness will give you a significant improvement in this leadership trait.

Intelligence as a Leadership Trait

Intelligence is something that can be difficult to develop. The road toward becoming more intelligent is difficult, long and can't be completed without investing considerable time. Developing intelligence is a lifestyle choice. Your college graduation was the beginning of your education, not the end. In fact, much of what is taught in college functions merely as a foundational language for lifelong educational experiences.

To develop intelligence you need to commit to continual learning–both formally and informally. With modern advances in distance education it is easy to take a class or two each year from well-respected professors in the evening at your computer.

Informally, you can develop a great deal of intelligence in any field simply by investing a reasonable amount of time to reading on a daily basis. The fact is that most people won't make a regular investment in their education. Spending 30 minutes of focused reading every day will give you 182 hours of study time each year.

For the most part, people will notice if you are intelligent by observing your behaviour and attitude. Trying to display your intelligence is likely to be counterproductive. One of the greatest signs of someone who is truly intelligent is humility. The greater your education, the greater your understanding of how little we really understand.

You can demonstrate your intelligence by gently leading people toward understanding–even when you know the answer. Your focus needs to be on helping others learn–not demonstrating how smart you are.

Arrogance will put you in a position where people are secretly hopeful that you'll make a mistake and appear foolish.

As unintuitive as it may seem, one of the best ways to exhibit intelligence is by asking questions. Learning from the people you lead by asking intelligent thoughtful questions will do more to enhance your intelligence credibility than just about anything. Of course this means you need to be capable of asking intelligent questions.

Everyone considers themselves intelligent. If you ask them to explain parts of their area of expertise and spend the time to really understand (as demonstrated by asking questions), their opinion of your intelligence will go up. After all, you now know more about what makes them so intelligent, so you must be smart as well. Your ability to demonstrate respect for the intellect of others will probably do more to influence the perception of your intellect than your actual intelligence. How often have you heard the comment, "He or she is a born leader?" There are certain characteristics found in some people that seem to naturally put them in a position where they're looked up to as a leader.

Whether in fact a person is born a leader or develops skills and abilities to become a leader is open for debate. There are some clear characteristics that are found in good leaders. These qualities can be developed or may be naturally part of their personality. Let us explore them further.

7 personal qualities found in a good Leader

1. A good leader has an exemplary character. It is of utmost importance that a leader is trustworthy enough to lead others. A leader needs to be trusted and be known to live their life with honestly and integrity. A good leader "walks the talk" and in doing so earns the right to take responsibility for others. True authority is born from respect for the good character and trustworthiness of the person who leads.

2. A good leader is enthusiastic about their work or cause and also about their role as leader. People will respond more openly to a person of passion and dedication. Leaders need to be able to be a source of inspiration, and be a motivator towards the required action or cause. Although the responsibilities and roles of a leader may be different, the leader needs to be seen to be part of the team working towards the goal. This kind of leader will not be afraid to roll up their sleeves and get dirty.

3. A good leader is confident. In order to lead and set direction, a leader needs to appear confident as a person and in the leadership

role. Such a person inspires confidence in others and draws out the trust and best efforts of the team to complete the task well. A leader who conveys confidence towards the proposed objective inspires the best effort from team members.

4. A leader also needs to function in an orderly and purposeful manner in situations of uncertainty. People look to the leader during times of uncertainty and unfamiliarity and find reassurance and security when the leader portrays confidence and a positive demeanour.

5. Good leaders are tolerant of ambiguity and remain calm, composed and steadfast to the main purpose. Storms, emotions, and crises come and go and a good leader takes these as part of the journey and keeps a cool head.

6. A good leader, as well as keeping the main goal in focus, is able to think analytically. Not only does a good leader view a situation as a whole, but is able to break it down into sub parts for closer inspection. While keeping the goal in view, a good leader can break it down into manageable steps and make progress towards it.

7. A good leader is committed to excellence. Second best does not lead to success. The good leader not only maintains high standards, but also is proactivein raising the bar in order to achieve excellence in all areas.

These seven personal characteristics are foundational to good leadership. Some characteristics may be more naturally present in the personality of a leader. However, each of these characteristics can also be developed and strengthened. A good leader whether they naturally possess these qualities or not, will be diligent to consistently develop and strengthen them in their leadership role.

Leadership is the uniquely consistent and defining force behind great, enduring organisations. All of the best strategies, creative ideas and brilliant game plans cannot succeed or be sustained without strong, effective leadership. Yet we severely diminish and trivialise leadership's true meaning by equating the word "leader" with any person in a position of authority or power.

Leadership is not something bestowed upon you or granted to you by virtue of your lofty title or set of responsibilities. Rather, true leadership is invited and can only be given willingly by others based on who you are, what you do and how you do it. Leadership is revealed by what you inspire and what you enable; that is, by your success in eliciting positive actions, emotions and behaviours in others without the promise of reward or threat of punishment, and in producing tangible outcomes through others.

Developing and possessing requisite skills and knowledge may help you attain a sought-after position of authority or power. But it is your character – the sum total of your values and beliefs reflected in your behaviours, actions and decisions – that others will judge before they truly agree to be led by you. Those who earn an invitation to lead others answer the question of character by choosing and exemplifying certain essential, non-negotiable qualities

Long time ago, there was a field technician named Daniel. This Youngman was recognised as having great technical skills and a good personality. He was known as a nice person and he received many compliments from both customers and fellow employees.

The company he worked for was expanding and a managerial position was available. He was offered and he accepted the position, even though he had no management experience and never really led anyone. He stated this to upper management, but they had the confidence he would pick it up due to his aptitude and attitude.

He knew that he would be faced with leadership challenges, and quickly found out that his decisions mattered. He focused too much on the small things which needed to be addressed but missed the big picture. He did not prioritise like he should have and tried to do everything himself so that he would not bother his staff. No one really knew the goals or objectives, or where the department was headed. He did all the talking because he thought that is what a leader is supposed to do. He thought the only way to get things done was to intimidate, and he would lose his temper when things did not go right. If anyone criticised him, he would become immediately defensive. He did not even think about motivating his staff, he thought they should just do the work they were getting paid for.

Although his staff respected his technical capabilities and liked him, they did not look at him as a leader. Once he talked to a couple of his closest staff members, he realised that he needed to take a good look at how he could improve. He thought about people he respected as leaders and realised that they never seemed to get upset and were usually calm. He found that he needed to build trust and make sure everyone saw the same vision for the future. He started meeting more with his staff and asking for their opinions and suggestions. He knew not to let criticism affect him personally, as everyone wants to succeed and enjoy their job at the same time. He realised the importance of proper multitasking and prioritisation. He made the decisions he was confident about, and asked key employees for help or confirmation whenever he was not 100% sure. He also started freeing up the responsibilities he held tight by delegating out tasks. His stress levels were decreasing and he started to act the part of a leader by being more calm and self-assured.

Even though he made some mistakes, and quite often would seek advice, he was earning trust from his team. This was due to always keeping them informed truthfully and never giving up until the issues were resolved. They felt he truly had things under control. He had their best interests at heart, and tried to motivate by mentoring, coaching and helping them grow. He listened to what they had to say and remained quiet until he had something useful or powerful to say. With this new humbled confidence, his leadership abilities improved to a point to where he was promoted to director and soon after, vice-president within the company.

What is the moral of this story?

This field technician with no management or leadership experience was able to grow once he realised the skills he needed in order to succeed. You as a leader, how do you relate with your followers? How do you respond when you are criticised? Do you prioritise? Do you seek to know exactly what the problem is? If you continue to do things yourself, you will wear yourself out. You are the leader to inspire them. Don't just go there dictating what they should do, you should let their opinions count as well. Discuss with them, share your view with them and let them suggest as well. You as the leader ought to earn respect, not demand it.

Some leaders don't even know how to earn respect. They just think as a leader they should just instruct and people must respond to them. Look at this man in the story, when he first started, he was doing everything himself and he refused to carry his followers along. But because of the love they had for him, they were honest with him when he came around. Oh yes! When he realised he wasn't getting anything done. They told him the truth. "Sir we appreciate you, we love you for all that you have been doing for the company, unfortunately, we don't see you as a true leader, because you are doing everything yourself. We don't even know the goals and objectives of the company". Some leaders would have felt somehow when they are advised like this. But this young man took the advice on board and worked on himself. He realised he's done so much to wrong them. He apologised to them, and then started doing things the way they were meant to be done. He thought about all the leaders he'd seen and those he loved so much. He tried to copy that which they're doing.

He realised that they don't get angry and that they're usually calm. As a leader, when you've done something wrong, do you always come clean by telling your followers that you are sorry? As a true leader, do you hold meetings with your followers or claim you don't have time? If you don't hold meetings there is no way you will know exactly what is going on. You won't be able to know the problems they are facing. You should let them see you as a true leader. They want to be inspired by you. They want to emulate you. They want you to be there for them. Some leaders are just too greedy thinking about themselves alone. They want everything for themselves.

-3-

What makes a true Leader?

Once upon a time, two princes were sent to train with a powerful vanguard in the mountains. Knowing the two were bitter rivals for the throne of their kingdom, the vanguard decided to do away with the joint exercises and let each boy camp out at opposite sides of the mountain.

Each day, the vanguard gave them a task to do and without telling the boys how their rival fared. At the end of the task, the vanguard would let each boy know if he did better by letting him get anything that he requested for. As a result, it became a blind competition between the two.

Mike, the younger of the two boys happened to be assigned to the western half of the mountain. The west side of the mountain, being exposed to the cool, damp winds made the vegetation lush and the fauna varied, making foraging easier. Soft wood made easy timber and water was never hard to come by. It was safe to assume for him that the other boy was having a harder time.

Then came the task;

On the first task, the boys were asked to build their own house. It was easy enough for Mike to find soft wood. He built a simple hut the first day but he had problems with the leaves he had used for roofing as they kept on falling off. Nonetheless, it was a sturdy house and the boy saw it was all good.

The vanguard came the next day and asked for what the boys wanted. Mike requested for rope to lash the roof leaves together. He got what he wanted.

On the next task, the boys were asked to gather food that would be enough to make them survive inside the houses for one week. The animals around Mike's house gave ample meat and he was able to gather them by the end of the day.

The vanguard came the next day and asked for what the boys wanted. Mike asked for salt to preserve the meat he had gathered as the meat was spoiling already, he got what he requested for.

The last task was to create a fortification around their houses. To that goal, Mike cut off very large trees and started pulling them up around the cabin. As the trees that he chose proved to be very heavy, he was only able to build half of the walling by the end of the day.

The vanguard came the next day and to Mike's surprise, still asked the boy what he wanted. Mike promptly asked for a lumber-cart to be able to finish the wall. The vanguard gave him what he wanted and left.

There were no more tasks left. All that was to it was to survive the week on what they already had. At that time, Mike started thinking, "If I was only able to half finish some of my tasks and still get my wish, my brother must be having a very hard time. I just have to survive to win this"

At the end of the week, the two brothers were given the signal to converge at the peak of the mountain. Even with the necessary preparations, life at the mountain was hard, meat spoiled, the roof leaked and the walls broke down. Mike arrived at the place badly bruised all over, in tattered clothes, and with empty stomach.

On the other hand, mike's brother arrived as though he had been there only that day, with a warm meat at hand, dry clothes and hardly any scratches on his skin.

Upon sight of this, Mike was outraged and started lashing it out on his sibling in front of the vanguard. "How can this be? Have we not been in the same mountain the whole week? Have I not fared better in every task? Brother, how dare you cheat behind my back?"

The brother did not speak. Instead, it was the vanguard who replied. "He didn't cheat and I never told anybody who won or lost each task"

"But I got my requests didn't i?" Mike replied with a grump

The brother still did not speak.

"In truth, you never won any of the tasks despite your advantage in terrain," explained the vanguard, "Funny as it may seem, every time I asked your brother what he wanted, he always asked me to fulfil your request because he didn't want you to lack any thing. Whereas, when I give what you've asked for to you, you always tell me you will like to keep the left-over so that your brother will not have anything"

Mike could no longer speak. Tears welled in the young boy's eyes.

"such is true leadership, being able to consider the fate of others around you despite the opportunity to take advantage to make the situation for your own betterment," said the vanguard as he declared the other brother the winner of the contest. Mike gracefully accepted defeat and the brothers made peace.

In our secular society we tend to think of a leader as a person who's well connected or who is powerful or charismatic or wealthy. We judge leaders by what they have. But a true leader should be judged by what he has not: Ego, arrogance, and self-interest. A true leader sees his work as a selfless service towards a higher purpose. As the sagists say leadership is not power and dominance. It is servitude. That doesn't mean that a leader is weak. He derives great strength from his dedication to a purpose that is greater than himself.

Every generation has its Moses, a leader who inspires absolute trust, who is totally dedicated to fulfilling his unique role. He understands and appreciates each person's role in perfecting this world and guides him or her accordingly. He rises above any individual perspective to take a global view, seeing how much each person and each issue fits into the entire scheme of the contemporary world.

A true leader will shake people from their reverie and tell them," No, you don't need to live a life of desperation and confusion. Yes, you do have the ability to find meaning in your life and the unique skills to fulfil that meaning. You're an important link in a chain of generations past. You have a legacy worth preserving and a future worth fighting for."

A true leader shows us that our world is indeed heading somewhere and that we control its movement. We need not be at the mercy of personal prejudices or prevailing political winds, none of us is subservient to the history or nature that we are history and nature. That we can rid the world of war, hate and ignorance, obliterate the borders that separate race from race and rich from poor.

A true leader does not seek followers. He wants to teach others how to be leaders. He doesn't want control. He wants truth. He doesn't impose his leadership on others, nor does he take away anyone's autonomy. He inspires by love, not coercion. When it comes time to take credit, he makes himself invisible. But he is the first to arrive at a time of need, and he will never shrink away in fear. He is so passionate about your welfare that when you consult him for guidance, it's like coming face to face with yourself for the first time.

How often do you as a leader check on your followers?

"Many years ago, a very strong woodcutter asked for a job with a timber merchant and he got it. The salary was really good and so were the work conditions. For that reason, the woodcutter was determined to do his best. The merchant showed him where he was supposed to work. The first day, the wood-cutter brought down 18 trees. "Congratulations," the merchant said. "Go on that way!"

Very motivated by the words of the timber merchant, the woodcutter tried harder the next day but could only bring down 15 trees. The third day, he tried even harder but could only bring down 10 trees. Day after day, he was bringing down less and less trees. "I must be losing my strength", the woodcutter thought.

He went to the timber merchant to apologise, he said he could not understand what was going on.

"When was the last time you sharpen your axe?" the timber merchant asked. "sharpen? I had no time to sharpen my axe. I have been busy trying to cut trees…"

A true leader will always check on his/ her followers to see what he/she is doing well and see if there are things he/she would need to improve on. A true leader will not just continue to lead without carrying out a check to see what they could do better. The woodcutter in this story did not have time to check on the tools he was using. Without checking on your followers as a leader you are only taking a walk.

Ways to identify bad Leaders

It's important to realise that just because someone holds a position of leadership, doesn't necessarily mean they should. Put another way, not all leaders are created equal. The problem many organisations are suffering from is a recognition problem – they can't seem to recognise good leaders from bad ones.

If I only had a nickel for every time I've been asked, "is there a simple test that can quickly determine an executive's leadership ability?" The short answer is" yes," but keep in mind, simple and fast aren't always the same thing as effective. There are a plethora of diagnostic tests, profiles, evaluations, and assessments that offer insights into leadership ability, or a lack thereof. My problem with these efforts is they are overly analytical, very theoretical, and very often subject to bias. That said, they are fast, easy, and relatively inexpensive. The good news is there is a better way to assess leadership ability. If you really want to determine someone's leadership prowess, give them some responsibility and see what they do with it. Leaders produce results. It's not always pretty, especially in the case of inexperienced leaders, but good leaders will find a way to get the job done.

If your enterprise has trouble identifying leaders, or has a shortage of leaders, you don't have a testing problem – you have a leadership problem. One of the primary responsibilities of leadership is to create more and better leaders. I believe it was John Maxwell who said, "there is no success without a successor."

Go ahead, test if you must, but paying attention to the following 15 items (listed in no particular order) will be much more practical, accurate, and effective. If your organisation has leaders who fail to grasp the concepts outlined below, you may want to stop testing them, ranking them, and promoting them – instead consider developing them or exiting them.

Leaders who can't see it probably won't find it: Leaders without vision will fail. Leaders who lack vision cannot inspire teams, motivate performance, or create sustainable value. Poor vision, tunnel vision, vision that is fickle, or a non-existent vision will cause leaders to fail. A leader's job is to align the organisation around a clear and achievable vision. This cannot occur when the blind lead the blind.

When leaders fail to lead themselves: A leader who lacks character or integrity will not endure the test of time. It doesn't matter how intelligent, affable, persuasive, or savvy a person is, if they are prone to rationalizing unethical behaviour based upon current or future needs, they will eventually fall prey to their own undoing. Optics over ethics is not a formula for success.

Put-up or shut-up: Nothing smacks of poor leadership like a lack of performance. Nobody is perfect, but leaders who consistently fail are not leaders, no matter how much you wish they were. While past performance is not always a certain indicator of future events, a long-term track record of success should not be taken lightly. Someone who has consistently experienced success in leadership roles has a much better chance of success than someone who has not. It's important to remember unproven leaders come with a high risk premium. Smart companies recognise potential, but they reward performance.

Beware! the know-it-all: The best leaders are acutely aware of how much they don't know. They have no need to be the smartest person in the room, but have the unyielding desire to learn from others. I've often said leaders who are not growing cannot lead a growing enterprise. One of the hallmarks of great leaders is their insatiable curiosity. If a leader isn't extremely curious about every aspect of their organisation, trust me when I say there are huge problems on the horizon.

Whenas a leader, you fail to communicate: When leaders are constantly flummoxed by those who don't seem to get it, there exists both a leadership and communications problem. Show me a leader with poor communication skills and I'll show you someone who will be short-lived in their position. Great leaders can communicate effectively across mediums, constituencies, and environments. They are active listeners, fluid thinkers, and know when to dial it up, down or off.

It's all about them: If a leader doesn't understand the concept of "service above self", they will not earn the trust, confidence, and loyalty of those they lead. Any leader is only as good as his or her team's desire to be led by them. An overabundance of ego, pride, and arrogance are not positive leadership traits. Real leaders take the blame and give the credit – not the other way around. Long story short - if a leader receives a vote of no-confidence from their subordinates…game over.

Love and leadership: While *love* and *leadership* are certainly two words you don't often hear in the same sentence, I can assure you that rarely does great leadership exist without love being present *and* practiced. In fact, if you examine failed leaders as a class, you'll find that a lack of love, misplaced love, or misguided love were contributing causes of said failures, if not the root cause. Empathy, humility and kindness are signs of leadership strength – not weakness.

One size fits all leadership style: The best leaders are fluid and flexible in their approach. They understand the power of and necessity for contextual leadership. "My way or the highway" leadership styles don't play well in today's world. It will result in a fractured culture, and ultimately a non-productive organisation. Only those leaders who can quickly recognise and adapt their methods to the situation at hand will be successful over the long haul. Think open-source not proprietary, surrender not control, and collaborate not dictate.

Lack of focus: Leadership is less about balance and more about priority. The best leaders are ruthless in their pursuit of focus. Those leaders who lack the focus and attention to detail needed to apply leverage and resources in an aggressive and committed fashion will perish. Leaders, who are not intentional and are not focused, will fail themselves and their team. Leaders who lack discipline will model the wrong behaviours and will inevitably spread themselves too thin. Organisations are at the greatest risk when leaders lose their focus. Intentions must be aligned with results for leaders to be effective.

Death by comfort zone: The best organisations beat their competition to the future, and the best leaders understand how to pull the future forward. Leaders satisfied with the status quo or those who tend to be more concerned about survival than growth won't do well over the long-run. The best leaders are focused on leading change and innovation to keep their organisations fresh, dynamic and growing. Bottom line – leaders who build a static business doom themselves to failure.

Not paying attention to the consumer: Leaders not attuned to the needs of the market will fail. As the old saying goes, if you're not taking care of your customers, someone else will be more than happy to. Successful leaders focus on the consumer experience, which in turn leads to satisfaction and loyalty. The best leaders find ways to consistently engage the consumer and incorporate them into their innovation and planning initiatives. If you ignore, mistreat or otherwise don't value your customer base, your days as a leader are most certainly numbered.

Get Invested: Leaders not fully committed to investing in those they lead will fail. The best leaders support their team, build into their team, mentor and coach their team and they truly care for their team. A leader not fully invested in their team won't have a team – at least not an effective one. Never forget the old saying; people don't care how much you know until they know how much you care – words to live by for leaders.

The "A" word: Real leaders are accountable. They don't blame others, don't claim credit for the success of their team, but always accept responsibility for failures that occur on their watch. Most of all, leaders are accountable to their team. I've always said that leaders not accountable totheir people will eventually be held accountable bytheir people.

It's the culture stupid: The lesson here is that culture matters – forget this and all other efforts with regard to talent initiatives will be dysfunctional, if not altogether lost. Don't allow your culture to evolve by default, create it by design. The first step in cultural design is to be very, very careful who you let through the front door. People, their traits, attitudes, and work ethic (or lacks thereof) are contagions. This can be positive or negative – the choice is yours. The old saying, "talent begets talent" is true, but talent that aligns with culture will produce better results than talent that does not.

Show some courage: Leadership devoid of courage is a farce. I'm not referring to arrogance or bravado, but real courage. It takes courage to break from the norm, challenge the status quo, seek new opportunities, cut your losses, make the tough decision, listen rather than speak, admit your faults, forgive the faults of others, don't allow failure to dampen your spirit, stand for those not capable of standing for themselves and to remain true to your core values. You can do none of these things without courage. Courage is having the strength of conviction to do the right thing when it would just be easier to do things right.

Leaders need to be honest, have a demonstrated track record of success, be excellent communicators, and place an emphasis on serving those they lead, be fluid in approach, and have laser focus and a bias toward action. If these traits are not possessed by your current leadership team or your emerging leaders, you will be in for a rocky road ahead.

Which of these traits stand out to you? Do you have any other signs of ineffective leaders worthy of mention?

-4-

Styles of Leadership

A couple of true stories:

The director of a community coalition understood her role clearly: to bring people and organisations together to work on common issues; to facilitate the work of the groups formed; and to support those who took on responsibility for the work. Her enthusiasm and hard work pulled coalition members onto committees and task forces and her skill at making people feel needed and valued kept them there. She sent cards of appreciation, thanking people for the work they were doing or had done and instituted a system of annual public awards to recognise those who had put in time and effort to improve the community. She even baked muffins for each coalition meeting. The result was that task forces retained their members over long periods of time and accomplished the work they had set out to do. The coalition was tremendously successful in addressing issues vital to the community, largely because of the director's effectiveness in bringing people together and making them feel valued.

The new high school principal was committed to excellence in teaching, and was convinced that the surest way to achieve it was to encourage teachers to take more control of their jobs and more ownership of the school. He wanted them to try out new ideas with students, to talk with one another about what they were doing, to establish mutual support systems and to participate in decision-making for the school. As he set out to change the school climate to make all this possible, he was surprised and dismayed to find that most teachers wanted no part of empowerment. They saw the administration and other teachers as threats, had no desire to innovate in their classrooms and wanted to get as far away as possible from teaching when they weren't actively engaged in it. After five years of frustrating effort, with only very modest success, the principal took another job in the system.

Both of these stories are about styles of leadership - the ways in which leaders see leadership and carry it out. Leadership styles can influence every action and every area of an organisation, from the nature of coffee breaks to the overall effectiveness of a community initiative. As a result, it's important to understand what different styles look like, which ones are more or less effective and how you can develop or change your style to come closer to the ideal you aspire to.

What is leadership style?

According to John Gardner, "Leadership is the process of persuasion or example by which an individual (or leadership team) induces a group to pursue objectives held by the leader or shared by the leader and his or her followers." If we accept that definition, then leadership style is the way in which that process is carried out.

Leaders' styles encompass how they relate to others within and outside the organisation, how they view themselves and their position and to a very large extent, whether or not they are successful as leaders. If a task needs to be accomplished, how does a particular leader set out to get it done? If an emergency arises, how does a leader handle it? If the organisation needs the support of the community, how does a leader go about mobilising it? All of these depend on leadership style.

Much of the materials in this book looks at individual leaders, but leadership can be invested in a team, or in several teams, or in different people at different times. Many, perhaps most organisations, have several levels of leadership, and thus many leaders. Regardless of the actual form of leadership, however, leadership style is an issue. Whether you're *the* leader of a large organisation or a member of a small group that practices collective leadership, the way that leadership plays out will have a great deal to do with the effectiveness and influence of your work.

Why pay attention to leadership style?

The style of an organisation's leadership is reflected in both the nature of that organisation and its relationships with the community. If a leader is suspicious and jealous of his power, others in the organisation are likely to behave similarly, in dealing with both colleagues and the community. If a leader is collaborative and open, she is likely to encourage the same attitudes among staff members, and to work collaboratively with other organisations.

In many ways, the style of its leader defines an organisation. If the organisation is to be faithful to its philosophy and mission, its leader's style must be consistent with them. An autocratic leader in a democratic organisation can create chaos. A leader concerned only with the bottom line in an organisation built on the importance of human values may undermine the purpose of its work. For that reason, being conscious of both your own style as a leader and those of others you hire as leaders can be crucial in keeping your organisation on the right track.

Conceptions and methods of leadership

We've all known and seen different types of leaders. One of the enduring images of the 20th century is that of hundreds of thousands of Germans wildly cheering their Fuhrer in Leni Riefenstahl's brilliant and terrifying 1930's Nazi propaganda film "Triumph of the Will." Franklin Roosevelt comforted a nation paralysed by economic depression by explaining that "We have nothing to fear but fear itself." John Kennedy electrified a generation with his exhortation to "Ask not what your country can do for you; ask what you can do for your country."

All of these are representations - for various purposes - of great motivational leaders working their magic through their speeches. Our concept of leadership tends to linger on such examples, but there are other kinds of leaders as well. Gandhi sitting and spinning in a dusty Indian courtyard; John Lewis and other Freedom Riders being brutally beaten in Mississippi; Vaclav Havel refusing to take revenge on the former Communist bureaucrats of Czechoslovakia; Nelson Mandela sitting in prison on Robben Island - these also are pictures of leadership.

Conceptions of leadership

The leadership style of an organisation may be concerned with less dramatic issues than these examples, but it nonetheless has profound effects on the people within that organisation and on everything the organisation does. Styles have to do with a leader's and an organisation's idea of what leadership is and does. Possible conceptions include:

- **Exercising power:** Leadership is a matter of pursuing one's own ends. Asserting power over others is an end in itself, and symbolises one's position as a leader.
- **Gaining and exercising the privileges of high status:** Leadership is about getting to the top, and being recognized as having the highest status.
- **Being the boss:** Leadership is overseeing the work of the organization by telling everyone what to do, when to do and rewarding or punishing as appropriate.
- **Task orientation:** Leadership is getting the job done - that's all that matters.
- **Taking care of people:** Leadership is looking out for those you lead, and making sure they get what they need.
- **Empowerment:** Leadership is helping those you lead gain power and become leaders.

Methods of leadership

In many or perhaps most organisations, more than one of these conceptions may define leadership. Each implies particular ways of leading and leaders may use a number of different methods.

- **Pure exercise of power**:. "My way or the highway." If you don't do what the leader demands, no matter how unreasonable, you're gone. The leader's decisions are not open to question or discussion and no one else gets to make decisions.

- **Political scheming:** The leader plays people off against one another, creates factions within the organisation, cultivates "allies" and isolates "enemies," and builds up (through favours or overlooking poor performance) personal debt which can be cashed in when needed, in order to manipulate people and events as he wishes.A school superintendent bragged to voters about how little was spent on the school system and then explained to teachers how they couldn't have raises because the community was too cheap to invest in education. He set principals at odds with one another and with teachers, played favourites among system administrators, postured in public, did his best to charm particular school committee members and generally kept everyone off balance. He did it so well that, for most of his long term of employment, almost no one noticed that he exercised no educational leadership whatsoever, and that the schools deteriorated both physically and educationally under his administration.

- **Using relationships:** The leader develops strong positive relationships with all or most of the people in the organisation and uses these relationships to steer people in particular directions. People do what they're asked because of their relationships with the leader, rather than for reasons connected to the tasks themselves.

- **Setting an example:** The leader may or may not demand or request particular behaviour or actions, but she will demonstrate them, and expect or imply that others will follow.In Sicily, a young archaeologist was the dig supervisor, given the task of negotiating with and organising local workmen for a dig. The workmen, most of them nearly twice the supervisor's age, saw the job as an opportunity to make some money without doing much work (and had been given to understand as much by the local Mafioso who recruited them).The supervisor surprised them by speaking their dialect and by treating them with respect. But the biggest surprise was that, after explaining carefully what needed to be done and how, he didn't stand over them or tell each person what to do. Instead, he simply turned away and went to work. The older men, impressed and embarrassed, started to work as well. They were surprised once more when they realised that the young archaeologist was willing to do any job, no matter how hard or dirty, and that, although they were farmers accustomed to labour, they couldn't outwork him no matter how they tried. Contrary to their original expectations, they worked hard for the time they were employed...without the supervisor ever giving orders.

- **Persuasion:** The leader convinces people through argument, reasoning, selling techniques, or other persuasive methods that what the leader wants is, in fact, the best course, or in line with what they want to do.

- **Sharing power**: Some leaders choose to exercise at least some leadership through the other stakeholders in the organisation. In this situation they may give up some personal power in return for what they see as more ownership of decisions, goals and the organisation itself by those involved in the decision-making process.

- **Charisma:** Some leaders are charismatic enough to simply pull others along by the power of their personalities alone. They may, in fact, advocate and accomplish wonderful things, but they do it through people's loyalty to and awe of them.Alexander the Great was only 18 when he succeeded his murdered father as King of Macedonia and only 32 when he died, but he was able in the short time in between to conquer much of the known world. His personal magnetism was such that his soldiers - who knew him well, and fought beside him - thought him immortal, and followed him for years through battle after battle and through one unknown country after another. As he lay dying, his whole army - 50,000 men - filed past to say goodbye personally to the leader they loved and revered. That's charisma.

- **Involving followers in the goal:** The leader gets others to buy into her vision for the organisation, and to make it their own. She may accomplish this through charisma, through the force of her own belief in the power and rightness of the vision or through the nature of the vision itself.

The combination of the leader's and organisation's conception of leadership and the leader's way of leading does much to define leadership style. In addition, the characteristics of the leadership are almost always reflected in the relationships within and among the staff, participants, Board and others related to the organisation, as well as in its policies, procedures, and programme. There are also other factors that come into play in defining leadership style. In some organisations, for instance, leaders are expected to shake things up, to foster and support change. In others, they are expected to sustain the statuesque. In some, they are expected to be proactive, and assertive; in others, more passive. All of these elements - concepts of leadership, methods of leading, attitude toward change, assertiveness - combine with personalities and individual experience in different ways to create different styles of leaders.

Keep in mind that each of the styles below is a stereotype that actually fits very few real people. Each is meant to outline the characteristics of a style in very simple and one-sided terms. Hardly anyone actually sees or exercises leadership as inflexibly as laid out here. Most leaders combine some of the characteristics of two or more of these styles, and have other characteristics that don't match any of those below. You can find many descriptions of other leadership styles as well. What this list really provides is some useful ways to think about your own and others' leadership.

It's also important to remember that people can be either effective or ineffective in any of these categories:

1. Autocratic. Autocratic leaders insist on doing it all themselves. They have all the power, make all the decisions and don't often tell anyone else about what they're doing. If you work for an autocratic leader, your job is usually to do what you're told.

An autocratic leader often maintains his authority by force, intimidation, threats, reward and punishment or position. Although he may or may not have a clear vision and may or may not be steering the organisation in the right direction, he's not concerned with whether anyone else agrees with what he's doing or not.

Autocratic leadership allows quick decision-making and eliminates arguments over how and why things get done. At the same time, however, it may reduce the likelihood of getting a range of different ideas from different people and can treat people badly or as if they don't matter. If, as is often true, the leader is concerned with his own power and status, he'll be looking over his shoulder and moving to squelch any opposition to him or his ideas and decisions. Innovation or the use of others' ideas is only permissible if it's part of the leader's plan.

Effects on the organisation. Autocratic leaders often leave fear and mistrust in their wake. Others in the organisation tend to copy the protection of their position and their distrust of others' ideas and motives. Often, autocratically -led organisations are not particularly supportive of personal relationships but much more keyed to chain-of-command. Everyone has her own sphere, and protects it at all costs. Communication tends to go in only one direction - up - as a result of which rumour can become the standard way of spreading news in the organisation.

At its best, autocratic leadership provides a stable and secure work environment and decisive, effective leadership. All too often, however, it can sacrifice initiative, new ideas and the individual and group development of staff members for the predictability of a highly structured, hierarchical environment where everyone knows exactly what he's supposed to do and follows orders without question.

Although the above paints a pretty bleak picture, many autocratic leaders are not hated and feared, but rather esteemed, and even loved. It depends on their own personalities - like anyone else, they can be nice people or highly charismatic or even willing to listen to and act on others' ideas - on the organisation itself (in the military, most soldiers want someone firmly in charge), on the quality of their decisions and on the needs of the people they lead. If they're generally decent and not abusive, make good decisions for the organisation and fulfil the parent-figure or authority-figure image that most people in the organisation are looking for, they can be both effective and well-respected.

2. Managerial: The leader who sees himself as a manager is concerned primarily with the running of the organisation. Where it's going is not an issue, as long as it gets there in good shape. He may pay attention to relationships with and among staff members, but only in the service of keeping things running smoothly. Depending upon the nature and stability of the organisation, his main focus may be on funding, on strengthening the organisation's systems and infrastructure (policies, positions, equipment, etc.) or on making sure day-to-day operations go well (including making sure that everyone is doing what he's supposed to).

If he's efficient, a managerial leader will generally be on top of what's happening in the organisation. Depending on the size of the Organisationand his management level, he'll have control of the budget, know the policies and procedures manual inside out, be aware of who's doing his job efficiently and who's not and deal with issues quickly and firmly as they come up. What he won't do is steer the organisation. Vision isn't his business; maintaining the organisation is.

Effects on the organisation: In general, a well-managed organisation, regardless of its leadership style, is a reasonably pleasant place to work. Staff members don't have to worry about ambiguity or about whether they'll get paid. As long as oversight is relatively civil - no screaming at people, no setting staff members against one another - things go along on an even keel. Good managers even try to foster friendly relationships with and among staff, because they make the organisation work better.

On the other hand, good management without a clear vision creates an organisation with no sense of purpose. The organisation may simply act to support the status quo, doing what it has always done in order to keep things running smoothly. That attitude neither fosters passion in staff members nor takes account of the changing needs (and they do change) of the target population or the community. The organisation may do what it does efficiently and well...but what it does may not be what it should be doing, and it won't be examining that possibility any time soon.

Obviously, the leader of any organisation - as well as any other administrator -has to be a manager at least some of the time. Many are in fact excellent managers and keep the organisation running smoothly on a number of levels. The issue here is the style that person adopts as a leader. If he sees management as his primary purpose, he's a managerial leader and will have a very different slant on leadership than if his style is essentially democratic, for instance.

3. Democratic: A democratic leader understands that there is no organisation without its people. He looks at his and others' positions in terms of responsibilities rather than status and often consults in decision-making. While he solicits, values and takes into account others' opinions; however, he sees the ultimate responsibility for decision-making as his own. He accepts that authority also means the buck stops with him. Although he sees the organisation as a cooperative venture, he knows that he ultimately has to face the consequences of his decisions alone.

Democratic leadership invites the participation of staff members and others, not only in decision-making, but in shaping the organisation's vision. It allows everyone to express opinions about how things should be done and where the organisation should go. By bringing in everyone's ideas, it enriches the organisation's possibilities. But it still leaves the final decisions about what to do with those ideas in the hands of a single person.

Some models of democratic leadership might put the responsibility in the hands of a small group - a management team or executive committee - rather than an individual.

Effects on the organisation: Democratic leadership, with its emphasis on equal status, can encourage friendships and good relationships throughout the organisation. (In more hierarchical organisations, clerical staff and administrators are unlikely to socialise, for instance; in a democratically-led organisation, such socialisation often happens). It helps people feel valued when their opinions are solicited and even more so if those opinions are incorporated into a final decision or policy.

What a democratic leadership doesn't necessarily do - although it can - is establish staff ownership of the organisation and its goals. Although everyone maybe asked for ideas or opinions, not all of those are used or incorporated in the workings of the organisation. If there is no real discussion of ideas, with a resulting general agreement, a sense of ownership is unlikely. Thus, democratic leadership may have some of the drawbacks of autocratic leadership - a lack of buy-in - without the advantages of quick and clear decision-making that comes with the elimination of consultation.

4. Collaborative. A collaborative leader tries to involve everyone in the organisation in leadership. He is truly first among equals, in that he may initiate discussion, pinpoint problems or issues that need to be addressed, and keep track of the organisation as a whole, rather than of one particular job. But decisions are made through a collaborative process of discussion, and some form of either majority or consensus agreement. Toward that end, a collaborative leader tries to foster trust and teamwork among the staff as a whole.

A collaborative leader has to let go of the need for control or power or status if he is to be effective. His goal is to foster the collaborative process and to empower the group - whether the staff and others involved in an organisation, or the individuals and organisations participating in a community initiative - to control the vision and the workings of the organisation. He must trust that, if people have all the relevant information, they'll make good decisions...and he must make sure that they have that information and provide the facilitation that assures those good decisions.

Effects on the organisation. Collaborative leadership comes as close as possible to ensuring that members of the organisation buy into its vision and decisions, since they are directly involved in creating them.

On the down side, management can be neglected in favour of building a collaborative organisation. Even more to the point, collaborative decision-making can be excruciating. Depending upon the group, ideas can be talked to death and insignificant disagreements about insignificant areas of policy can take hours to resolve.

Collaborative decision-making can be democratic - based on a majority vote after discussion - or dependent on arriving at consensus, with a range of possibilities in between. Consensus decision-making is particularly difficult, in that it requires everyone to agree before a decision can be made. A single determined individual can derail the process indefinitely. Even at its best, a consensus process can take inordinate amounts of time and try the patience of all involved. It's not impossible to employ but it takes real commitment to the ideal of consensus and enormous patience. In practice, true consensus decision-making is most often used in collective organisations, which are significantly different from collaborative ones and often involve everyone in leadership.

-5-

Another way of looking at Leadership style

A different view, popularised by James McGregor Burns, contrasts two styles of leadership: transactional and transformational.

Transactional leadership, as its name implies, views leadership as based on transactions between leader and followers. The leader sees human relations as a series of transactions. Thus rewards, punishments, reciprocity, exchanges (economic, emotional, and physical) and other such "transactions" are the basis of leadership. In simplest terms, I lead this organisation by paying you and telling you what you need to do; you respond by doing what you need to do efficiently and well and the organisation will prosper.

Transformational leadership looks at leadership differently. It sees a true leader as one who can distil the values and hopes and needs of followers into a vision and then encourage and empower followers to pursue that vision. A transactional leader thinks of improvement or development as doing the same thing better: an organisation that reaches more people, a company that makes more money. A transformational leader thinks about changing the world, even if only on a small scale.

Combining the two views of leadership style

These two ways of looking at leadership style are not mutually exclusive; in fact, it's easier to look at leadership in the context of both. Assuming, as almost all leadership theorists do, that transformational is either better than, or a necessary addition to, transactional leadership, what elements go into creating a transformational leader?

What styles are transformational leaders likely to employ and how?

Elements of transformational leadership

The transformational leader conceives of leadership as helping people to create a common vision and then to pursue that vision until it's realised. He elicits that vision from the needs and aspirations of others, gives it form and sets it up as a goal to strive for. The vision is not his: it is a shared vision that each person sees as his own.

Martin Luther King's overwhelming "I have a Dream" speech derived its power not only from the beauty of his oratory, but from the fact that it crystalised the feelings of all those citizens, of all races, who believed that racism was a great wrong. In that speech, King spoke with the voices of the hundreds of thousands who stood before the Lincoln Memorial and of millions of others who shared in his vision. That speech remains as the defining moment of the Civil Rights struggle and defined King - who had already proved his mettle in Birmingham and elsewhere - as a transformational leader.

The concept behind transformational leadership is thus providing and working toward a vision, but also has elements of empowerment, of taking care of people and even of task orientation. The job of the transformational leader is not simply to provide inspiration and then disappear. It is to be there, day after day, convincing people that the vision is reachable, renewing their commitment, priming their enthusiasm. Transformational leaders work harder than anyone else and in the words of a spiritual, "keep their eyes on the prize".

The methods that transformational leaders might use to reach their goals can vary. They'll virtually always include involving followers in the goal, as well as charisma, which comes, if not from personal characteristics, from the ability to put a mutual vision into words and to move a group toward the realization of that vision. Transformational leaders may also use sharing power, setting an example and/or persuasion to help move a group toward its goal.

What style does all that imply? The managerial style is perhaps least appropriate to transformational leadership, since it pays no attention to vision. The autocratic pays little attention to the ideas of others and is not generally congenial to the transformational leader. On the other hand, there was Hitler, who tapped into the deepest emotions of those he led and voiced them in a frightening but highly effective way. There is no guarantee that a transformational leader will work for the betterment of humanity, or at least couch his vision in those terms. The intersection of the transformational and the autocratic is not impossible but it usually has, at best, mixed results.

Fidel Castro initiated and has maintained desperately-needed land, education, health, and other reforms in Cuba, for which he is still revered by much of the island's population. He also eliminated any vestige of political freedom, imprisoned and executed dissenters and political opponents and was at least partially responsible for destroying much of Cuba's economic base in the name of ideological purity. As with the four styles described earlier, there is no guarantee that either a transactional or transformational leader will be an effective one.

The democratic and collaborative styles are both better possibilities for transformational leadership. Both allow for input from everyone and both encourage participation in the realization of long-term goals. It can be difficult for a highly motivated, charismatic leader to operate in the collaborative mode, but it can also be tremendously satisfying. There is an argument to be made that, because of the high degree of ownership of the vision in a collaboratively-run organisation, the collaborative style could be the most successful for transformational leadership. As noted above, David Chrislip and Carl Larson actually see collaborative and transformational leadership as essentially the same.

How do you determine what is an appropriate style?

All that said, it is probably true that any leader, even a highly collaborative one, uses a range of different styles at different times -

even, perhaps, in the course of a single day. Decisions have to be made, major and minor crises have to be sorted out, situations and conflicts have to be resolved, often right at the moment. It is important to realise that different styles may be appropriate at different times and for different purposes.

In an emergency, no one would suggest sitting down and making a group decision about what to do. There has to be decisive action and one person has to take it as soon as possible. As long as it's clear who that person is, there should be no question about the philosophical issues involved. By the same token, it's counter -productive to make decisions about how people should do their jobs without at least consulting those people about what might work best. Good leaders usually have a style that they consciously use most of the time, but they're not rigid. They change as necessary to deal with whatever comes up.

There are at least two other factors that have to be considered when choosing leadership style. The first is that leadership style - at least at the beginning - must, to at least some extent, be consistent with what people in the organisation expect. You can try to change their expectations and perceptions of how an organisation should be run - that's part of leadership - but you have to start by meeting them at least halfway or you'll never get close enough to talk about it.

If you're trying to turn a system that's been autocratic into a collaborative one, you have to accept that most people in the system not only won't welcome the change and that some won't even understand what you're suggesting. You also have to accept that they've probably developed their own methods of getting around the rigidity of the system that they'll continue to use, even if the system is no longer rigid. It can take a long time just to get your ideas across and longer to help people overcome their suspicions and break old habits. A few may never be able to. You need patience and the willingness to act occasionally in ways you'd rather not.

In the second story, the school principal was on the side of the angels: he was trying to be a collaborative, transformational leader who would inspire and support teachers to become the best educators they could and who would make the school into a model of excellence, learning for all and collegiality. The problem was that the teachers expected something entirely different. They wanted someone to tell them what to do and then leave them alone to do it. They saw the principal's plans as just another way to trick them into doing things they didn't want to do and to get them to work longer hours. The more he tried to explain how what he was asking was for their benefit, the more they resisted - they'd heard that *line* before.

If he had started where the teachers were, the principal might have been able to be more successful. That would have meant his "running" the school as his predecessor had, and introducing reforms slowly over a long period. Suggestions to receptive teachers might have started the process; professional development could have helped it along. He might have used incentives of some sort to encourage teachers to try new things, rather than assuming they would be happy to be more independent and creative. Paying attention to the expectations of the staff might have paid off for the principal in the long run.

Your style needs to be consistent with the goals, mission, and philosophy of your organisation. As mentioned earlier ,- an organisation cannot remain faithful to its mission if its internal structure is at odds with its guiding principles. An organisation dedicated to empowerment of the target population, for instance, must empower its staff as well. For most grass roots and community-based organisations, this consistency would mean using some variation of a democratic or collaborative style.

-6-

ℋow do you choose and develop a Leadership style?

What kind of leader do you want to be? Perhaps even more important, how would you be most effective as a leader? What kind of leadership style would be of the most benefit to your organisation and would allow you to be the best leader you could be? The leadership styles described in this book aren't the only ways to look at leadership. As we've already discussed, most real leaders use a combination of styles and there are others that haven't really been touched on here.

It's possible that Alexander the Great was a born leader but how much are you like Alexander the Great? Be honest now...it's doubtful, isn't it? Just about all leaders, even great leaders, have to learn how to lead and have to develop their skills over a period of time. You can do the same, especially if you have a clear idea of what you think leadership is about and if you have good models to learn from. Here are a few things you can do to choose and develop your own effective leadership style:

1. Start with yourself: Use what you know about your own personality, and about how you've exercised leadership in the past. Neither of these has to determine what you choose now - people can change, especially if they believe that what they've done before was ineffective or inconsistent with their values - but it's important to be honest with yourself about who you are. That honesty has two aspects.

First, be clear with yourself about what your natural tendencies and talents are. If you want to be a collaborative leader, but you tend to tell people what to do, you have to admit that and think about ways to change it. If you want to be a directive leader but you have trouble making decisions, you need to deal with that issue. Not everyone can be charismatic but almost everyone can learn to distil and communicate a vision that reflects the hopes and needs of a group. Knowing who youare is the first step toward both choosing a style and understanding what you'll have to do to adopt it.

Being truly honest with yourself is a difficult task. For most of us, it may take some time with a counsellor or a trusted friend or the willingness to hear feedback from colleagues, co-workers, and/or family members. It also takes honest self -assessment, which can mean stripping away defences and facing insecurities.

Some questions you might ask yourself to start:

i. How great is my need to be in control? (When you're in a car, are you uncomfortable if you're not driving, assuming the driver is competent? Would you let someone else order for you in a restaurant? If you were teaching a class, would it be a lecture? Would you follow tangents that were interesting to class members? Is there a right way to do most things? If your answers to these questions are yes, no, yes, no, and yes, you probably have a pretty high need to be in control of things.)

ii. How willing am I to trust others to do their jobs? (Are you uncomfortable delegating work, so that you just try to do it yourself? Do you tell people exactly how to do things, even when they have experience doing them? Do you think supervisors should spend a lot of their time checking the work of those they supervise? "Yes" answers to these questions could mean that you don't have much confidence in others.)

iii. How patient am I? (If someone is having trouble doing something, do you just do it for him? Do you interrupt with your comments before others have finished speaking? Do you want the discussion to end because you want to start doingsomething? If all these are the case, patience may not be your greatest virtue.)

iv. How organised am I? (Can you almost always find whatever you need without having to search for it? Is your desk clean? Are your files alphabetized and orderly? Are your books alphabetized? Do you have a place for nearly everything? Is your appointment book readable by anyone but you? Are you always on time, and hardly ever miss appointments?)

v. How good are my people skills? Are you comfortable with other people? Do people seem comfortable with you? When you're with others, do you spend most of your time talking? Listening? About even? Do people seek you out for help or advice? Do you consider yourself a good judge of people, and has that been borne out by your experience? Do you try to consider others' needs and feelings in any decision?

These few questions are obviously just a beginning, but they should help you think about some important leadership issues. If you have a high need for control, for instance, it doesn't mean you can't be a collaborative leader, but it does mean that you'll have to learn some new behaviour and perhaps a whole new way of looking at things. If you're not well-organised, it doesn't mean you can't be a good manager, but you'll have to find strategies to keep you on top of everything.

Acknowledge and be true to your beliefs. If you have a real philosophical commitment to a particular leadership style, it will probably be easier for you to change your behaviour to match that style than to live with knowing you're betraying your principles.

2. Think about the needs of the organisation or initiative. A community coalition almost has to have collaborative leadership or it will fall apart amid turf issues and accusations of discrimination. An organisation that responds to situations where it has to act quickly - an emergency medical team, for example, may need more decisive and directive leadership. Some groups may have an impassioned vision, but don't have the practical skills - financial management, scheduling, etc. - to achieve it.

You can adapt most styles to most situations, but don't neglect the real needs of the organisation in your calculations. You may need to practice a different style at the beginning from the one that you want to assume over the long term, in order to solve problems in the organisation or to get people on board. As it's the case in the story of the principal.for instance, the school principal might have had more success if he had started by making very little change and moved more slowly into the role and philosophy he wanted.

3. Observe and learn from other leaders. Think about how leaders you've worked for or with exercised leadership. What were their styles and were they effective? How did they handle different kinds of situations? How did what they did make you and others feel? Try to watch others in action and talk to them about how they see what they do. What do you like about how they operate? What don't you like? What can you incorporate into your own style?

Find a mentor. If there's a leader whom you particularly admire, and that person is accessible. Talk with him about leadership issues - about how he perceives what he's doing, how he'd handle particular situations and why, etc. Most people, especially if they're good leaders and conscious of what they do and why, would welcome the opportunity to help others develop their own leadership skills.

4. Use the research on leadership. There are lots of resources available on leaders and on both the theory and practice of leadership. They'll give you a lot more ideas about leadership styles and help you refine your own thinking about what leadership is and what kind of leader you'd like to be.

5. Believe in what you're doing. If you've thought it through carefully, and believe in the way you practice leadership that will be projected to others. If you believe in yourself, they'll believe in you, too.

6. Be prepared to change. Although this may seem at odds with some of the above, it is probably the most important element to good leadership. No matter how well you're doing, it's not perfect - it never is and never will be. Be prepared to find for yourself or hear from others the negative as well as the positive, to consider it carefully and objectively and to make corrections if necessary. That way, you can not only become a good leader but continue to be one.

In Summary:

Leadership style is the way in which a leader accomplishes his purposes. It can have profound effects on an organisation and its staff members, and can determine whether the organisation is effective or not.

Leadership style depends on the leader's and organisation's conception of what leadership is and on the leader's choice of leadership methods. Depending on how these fit together, a leader might adopt a variety of styles, each reflective of the way the organisation operates and the way its staff members relate to one another.

10 Common leadership and management mistakes

1. Lack of Feedback

Sarah is a talented sales representative but she has a habit of answering the phone in an unprofessional manner. Her boss is aware of this but he's waiting for her performance review to tell her where she's going wrong. Unfortunately, until she's been alerted to the problem, she'll continue putting off potential customers.

According to 1,400 executives polled by The Ken Blanchard Companies, failing to provide feedback is the most common mistake that leaders make. When you don't provide prompt feedback to your people, you're depriving them of the opportunity to improve their performance.

To avoid this mistake, learn how to provide regular feedback to your team.

2. Not Making Time for Your Team

When you're a manager or leader, it's easy to get so wrapped up in your own workload that you don't make yourself available to your team.

Yes, you have projects that you need to deliver. But your people must come first – without you being available when they need you, your people won't know what to do and they won't have the support and guidance that they need to meet their objectives.

Avoid this mistake by blocking out time in your schedule specifically for your people and by learning how to listen actively to your team. Develop your emotional intelligence so that you can be more aware of your team and their needs and have a regular time when "your door is always open", so that your people know when they can get your help. Once you're in a leadership or management role, your team should always come first - this is, at heart, what good leadership is all about!

3. Being Too "Hands-Off"

One of your team has just completed an important project. The problem is that he misunderstood the project's specification and you didn't stay in touch with him as he was working on it. Now, he's completed the project in the wrong way and you're faced with explaining this to an angry client.

Many leaders want to avoid micro-management. But going to the opposite extreme (with a hand-offs management style) isn't a good idea either – you need to get the right balance.

4. Being Too Friendly

Most of us want to be seen as friendly and approachable to people in our team. After all, people are happier working for a manager that they get on with. However, you'll sometimes have to make tough decisions regarding people in your team and some people will be tempted to take advantage of the relationship if you're too friendly with them.

This doesn't mean that you can't socialise with your people. But, you do need to get the balance right between being a friend and being the boss.Learn how to avoid this mistake. Also, make sure that you set clear boundaries, so that team members aren't tempted to take advantage of you.

5. Failing to Define Goals

When your people don't have clear goals, they muddle through their day. They can't be productive if they have no idea what they're working for or what their work means. They also can't prioritise their workload effectively, meaning that projects and tasks get completed in the wrong order.

Avoid this mistake by learning how to set smart goals for your team. Use a teamCharter to specify where your team is going and detail the resources it can draw upon. Also, use principles from 'Objectives 'to align your team's goals to the mission of the organisation.

6. Misunderstanding Motivation

Do you know what truly motivates your team? Here's a hint: chances are, it's not just money!

Many leaders make the mistake of assuming that their team is only working for monetary reward. However, it's unlikely that this will be the only thing that motivates them. For example, people seeking a greater work/life balance might be motivated by telecommuting days or flexible working. Others will be motivated by factors such as achievement, extra responsibility, praise or a sense of camaraderie.

7. Hurrying Recruitment

When your team has a large workload, it's important to have a full team. But filling a vacant role too quickly can be a disastrous mistake.

Hurrying recruitment can lead to recruiting the wrong people for your team: people who are uncooperative, ineffective or unproductive. They might also require additional training and slow down others on your team. With the wrong person, you'll have wasted valuable time and resources if things don't work out and they leave. What's worse, other team members will be stressed and frustrated by having to "carry" the under-performer.

You can avoid this mistake by learning how to recruit effectively, and by being particularly picky about the people you bring into your team.

8. Not "Walking the Walk"

If you make personal telephone calls during work time or speak negatively about your CEO, can you expect people on your team not to do this too? Probably not!As a leader, you need to be a role model for your team. This means that if they need to stay late, you should also stay late to help them. Or, if your organisation has a rule that no one eats at their desk, then set the example and head to the break room every day for lunch. The same goes for your attitude – if you're negative some of the time, you can't expect your people not to be negative.

So remember, your team is watching you all the time. If you want to shape their behaviour, start with your own. They'll follow suit.

9. Not Delegating

Some managers don't delegate, because they feel that no-one apart from themselves can do key jobs properly. This can cause huge problems as work bottlenecks around them and as they become stressed and burned out.

Delegation does take a lot of effort up-front and it can be hard to trust your team to do the work correctly. But unless you delegate tasks, you're never going to have time to focus on the "broader-view" that most leaders and managers are responsible for. What's more, you'll fail to develop your people so that they can take the pressure off you.

10. Misunderstanding Your Role

Once you become a leader or manager, your responsibilities are very different from those you had before.

However, it's easy to forget that your job has changed and that you now have to use a different set of skills to be effective. This leads to you not doing what you've been hired to do – leading and managing.

Key Points

We all make mistakes, and there are some mistakes that leaders and managers make in particular. These includes, not giving good feedback, being too "hands-off," not delegating effectively, and misunderstanding your role.

It's true that making mistakes can be a learning opportunity. But, taking the time to learn how to recognise and avoid common mistakes can help you become productive and successful and highly respected by your team.

www.ingramcontent.com/pod-product-compliance
Lightning Source LLC
Chambersburg PA
CBHW021900170526
45157CB00005B/1895